THE CHRISTIAN ADVENTURE

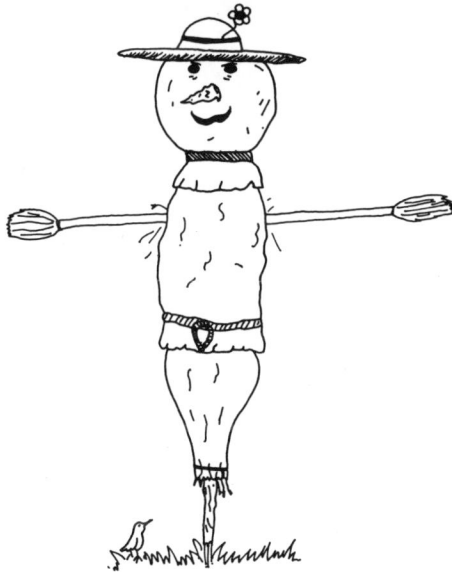

The Christian Adventure

A YOUNG PERSON'S GUIDE TO THE CHRISTIAN LIFE

Mike Fox and Sue Doggett
with illustrations by the children of Reigate

⬤▶❯ The Bible Reading Fellowship

Published by
The Bible Reading Fellowship
Peter's Way
Sandy Lane West
Oxford
OX4 5HG
ISBN 0 7459 3070 0
Albatross Books Pty Ltd
PO Box 320
Sutherland
NSW 2232
Australia
ISBN 0 7324 0908 X

First edition 1995

Acknowledgments
Scriptures quoted from the Good News Bible published
by The Bible Societies/HarperCollins Publishers Ltd., UK
© American Bible Society, 1966, 1971, 1976, 1992,
with permission.

Cover picture: Zefa (UK)

A catalogue record for this book is available
from the British Library

Printed and bound in Malta

CONTENTS

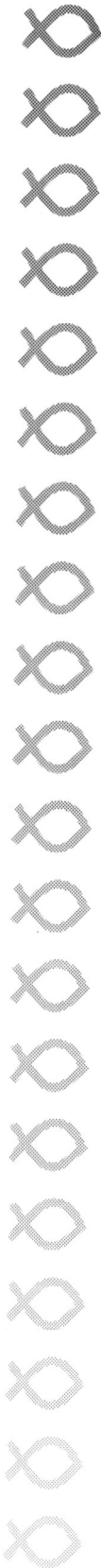

With lots of thanks to everyone in Reigate who helped with all the pictures, especially Mary who got them sorted out.

BEING A CHRISTIAN can be *FUN!*

will often be *EXCITING!*

may be *PACKED WITH ACTION!*

Best of all *BEING A CHRISTIAN IS A GREAT ADVENTURE!*

We have written this little book for you, with the help of some young people, so that you can understand what a Christian is and how you can become one.

We hope you enjoy reading it!

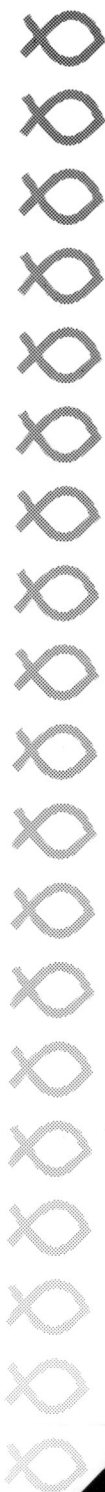

1

Y ou can read this book on
your own or with a friend or
with an older person to help you.

Before you start reading here is a
prayer you can pray:

Dear God,
please help me to understand more about how I
can join in the adventure of being a Christian.
For Jesus' sake. Amen.

GOD IS ALWAYS LISTENING

WHAT IS A CHRISTIAN?

F irst of all, what do you think a Christian is? Do you think, for instance, that it's someone who goes to church? Well, Christians do go to church—but a Christian isn't just someone who goes to church.

After all, you can go to a stable—but that doesn't make you a horse!

Would you say that a Christian is someone who tries hard to be good? Well, a Christian does try to be good, but a Christian isn't just someone who tries hard to be good.

Lots of people try and try and try—but it doesn't always seem to work!

Ah, you might say, then it must mean someone who was baptized (or christened) as a baby! Well, some Christians were baptized when they were babies, but a Christian isn't just someone who was christened as a baby.

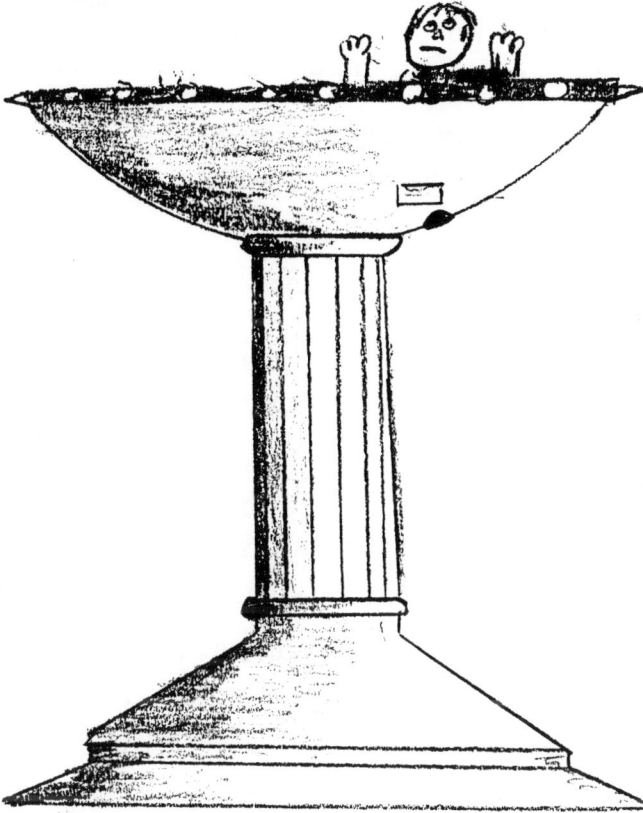

People who are baptized as babies have promises made for them. But being a Christian means making those promises for yourself.

GREAT NEWS!

W ell, if being a Christian is none of these things by themselves, what is a Christian?

> THE BIBLE TELLS US THAT BEING A CHRISTIAN IS **GREAT NEWS!**

What do you know about the Bible?

Christians call the Bible 'the word of God' because it tells us all about God's plan for his world.

The Bible is like a map which points the way to God.

The Bible isn't just one book—it's a collection of 66 books and it's divided into two parts:

The first part is the 'Old Testament' (this was written before Jesus lived on earth).

The second part is the 'New Testament' (this was written after Jesus' life on earth).

To help you find your way around the Bible each book within it is divided into chapters and each chapter is divided into verses.

If you don't yet have a Bible of your own you could buy one from a bookshop or ask for one as a birthday or Christmas present. Ask for the Good News Bible, which is quite easy to read. Be proud of your Bible and treat it with care.

GOOD NEWS BIBLE

IN THE BEGINNING...

What do you know about God?

This is how the Bible begins:

'In the beginning......God created the universe....'

Look around you at the world God has made.
The sky, the sea, and the earth. The sun, the moon
and the stars. The trees, the flowers and the living
creatures.

MC. DONALDS

God made everything!

The Bible also tells us that 'God
looked at everything he had
made and he was very pleased'.

God loves everything he made!

And best of all... God loves you!

*T*he Bible tells us what God is like. How many different descriptions of God can you find in this wordsearch? There are 17 words in the search altogether.

Some are written forward, some backwards and some diagonally. Can you find them all? Can you think of any more words which would describe God?

```
F L U F I C R E M P Q M
A E F A I T H F U L I T
G N I V I G R O F G P R
N U Y E F A I R H T E U
O R B X R A R T O N R T
R T Z H O L Y J P E F H
T R I G H T A U L I E F
S K S G O O D S U T C U
N E A R R W V T T A T L
P O W E R F U L H P E S
G N I V O L S E K I N D
E G N I T S A L R E V E
```

ANSWERS

merciful, faithful, truthful, forgiving, mighty, right, kind, patient, perfect, loving, good, strong, everlasting, fair, near, powerful, holy

God says: There is no other god, I am the only God there is.

Isaiah 45:21–22

8

When we look around us, we can see the world and the living things that God has made, but we can't see God in the same way that we can see each other. Here are some of the things that the Bible tells us about God:

God is like a very kind father who adores his children.

God is like a very wise king who cares for his people.

God is like a very good shepherd who watches over his sheep.

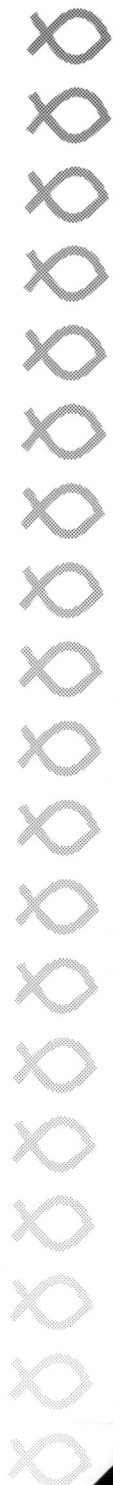

Yuu can get to know God as you look around you at all the good things he has made.

People like to say 'thank you' to God by praising him.

Lots of the songs that people sing in church are songs that say 'thank you' to God and are songs which praise him.

'I will praise you, Lord, with all my heart;
I will tell of all the wonderful things you
have done.
I will sing with joy because of you.
I will sing praise to you, Almighty God!'

Psalm 9:1–2

10

God loves to hear us praising him

*not because he is a big show-off
but because he is*

THE GOD OF THE WHOLE UNIVERSE

*The Lord is great and is to be highly praised...
As long as I live I will sing praises to my God...
Praise the Lord, all living creatures!
Praise the Lord!*

Psalm 96:4; 104:33; 150:6

11

God loves us to talk to him, just as we talk to each other.

Talking to God is called 'prayer'.

A very famous prayer is the Lord's Prayer which is the prayer that Jesus taught to his friends.

You can use the Lord's Prayer when you talk to God.

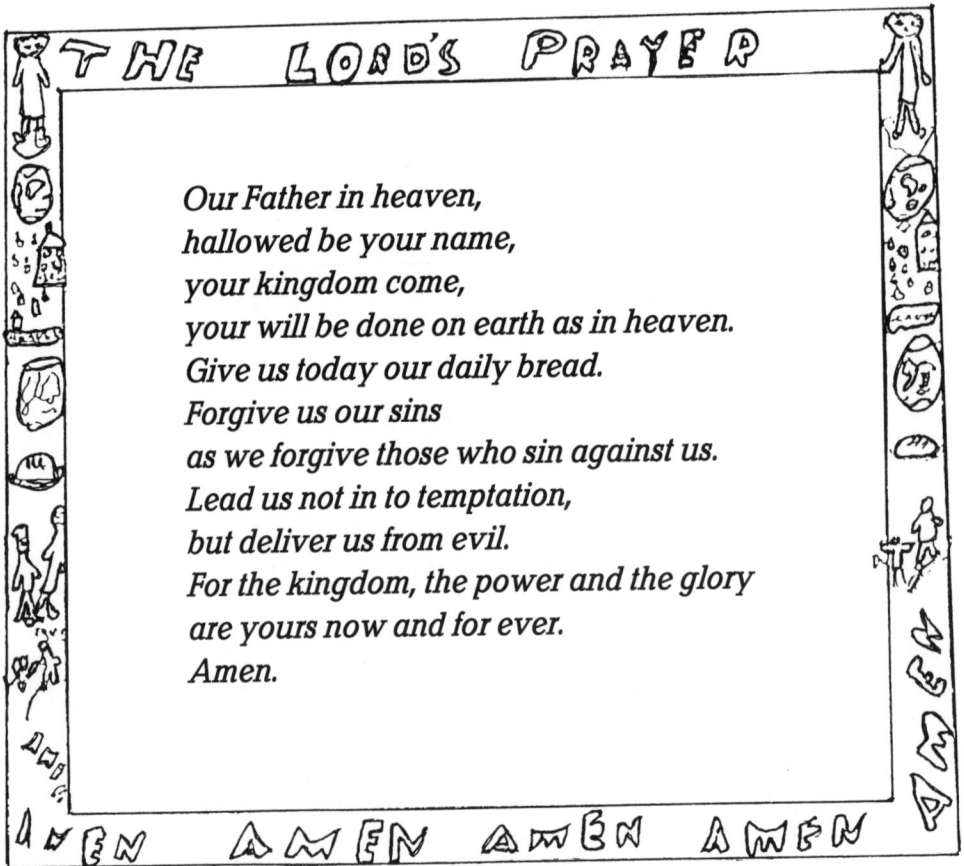

THE LORD'S PRAYER

Our Father in heaven,
hallowed be your name,
your kingdom come,
your will be done on earth as in heaven.
Give us today our daily bread.
Forgive us our sins
as we forgive those who sin against us.
Lead us not in to temptation,
but deliver us from evil.
For the kingdom, the power and the glory
are yours now and for ever.
Amen.

AMEN AMEN AMEN AMEN

GOD'S SON..

W hat do you know about Jesus?

Jesus is God's Son. God sent an angel to Mary to tell her that he had chosen her to be Jesus' mother.

CHRISTMAS

Jesus was born in a place called Bethlehem. Mary and her husband, Joseph, knew that God had chosen them for the special task of looking after the baby Jesus and caring for him as he grew up.

You can read all about Jesus' life on earth in the four Gospels: Matthew, Mark, Luke and John.

13

When he was grown up Jesus spent his life on earth helping and serving people.

He taught them about God.

People used to rush up to him and crowd round him, eager to listen to what he was saying.

He told them stories.

He explained things well, so that people understood. And he had a good sense of humour.

He did wonderful things for people.

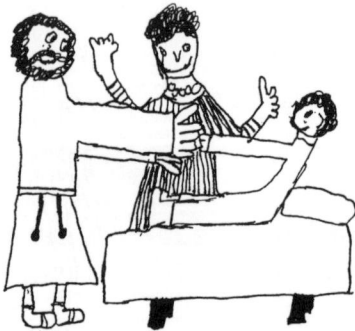

He helped them, and made them well when they were sick. He was their friend, even when other people disliked them.

Most of all, Jesus showed people what
God is really like.

He taught them how much God loved
them and how sad God was when they
did bad things.

And he explained that he was the Son of God—
that God was his Father. He then explained
that God is our Father, too.

*B*ut not everyone was pleased about what Jesus was doing and saying. Some of the more powerful people were jealous of him and they didn't like it when he said that he was God's Son.

They arrested Jesus because they thought he was misleading the people by claiming to be the Son of God. And they sentenced Jesus to death. They killed God's Son!

GOOD FRIDAY

But that was not the end of the story . . .

W hen people make mistakes they often say 'No one's perfect'. Well, that's true!

But God is perfect.
(Did you spot that in the word search descriptions of God?)

Because he is God's Son, Jesus knows that although God loves us, the fact that we're not perfect makes
it difficult for us to be friends with God.

You could say that there is a

big gap

between us and God.
Jesus is the only one who can

bridge that gap.

The Bible says:

... God has shown us how much he loves us ... he made us his friends through the death of his Son.

Romans 5:8, 10

17

When Jesus died he didn't die because he had done anything wrong, he died willingly so that we could be forgiven for all the things we've done wrong.

This wasn't easy for Jesus to do but he chose to do it. He did it because he loved us very much. He wanted us to be able to live with God for ever.

W hen Jesus died he made it possible for us to be friends with God.

Then something very special happened after Jesus had died. Three days later he rose from the dead.

The Bible tells us that many people saw Jesus after he rose from the dead. He wasn't a ghost. He ate with them and talked to them.

Jesus wanted his friends to understand that they could now be friends with God and he asked them to tell everyone the GREAT NEWS!

Jesus' friends were the first Christians. They did what Jesus asked and told everyone about what Jesus had done. (With a little bit of help from someone special, as you'll see on page 22!)

The Bible tells us the story of that first Easter:

Very early on Sunday morning the women went to the tomb . . . They found the stone rolled away . . . so they went in; but they did not find the body of the Lord Jesus. They stood there puzzled about this, when suddenly two men in bright shining clothes stood by them. Full of fear, the women bowed down to the ground, as the men said to them, 'Why are you looking among the dead for one who is alive? He is not here; he has been raised.'

Luke 24:1–6

Jesus' friend Peter 'ran to the tomb; he bent down and saw the linen wrappings but nothing else. Then he went back home amazed at what had happened.'

Luke 24:12

Jesus says: 'I am the living one! I was dead, but now I am alive for ever and ever.'

Revelation 1:18

When Jesus died he made it possible for God to forgive us for all the bad things we say, think and do. When he rose again he made it possible for us to be friends with God for ever.

Jesus is alive today

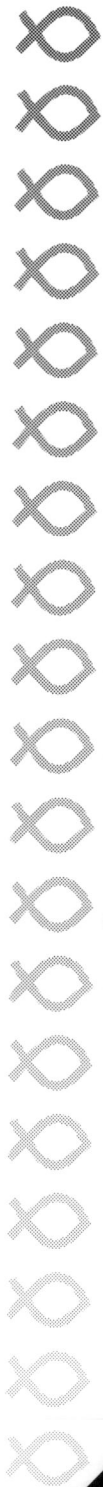

HELP ON THE WAY...

W hat do you know about the Holy Spirit?

A few weeks after he had risen from the dead, Jesus told his friends that he was going back to heaven to be with God, his Father.

He knew his friends couldn't manage on their own so he told them that he would send his Holy Spirit to live with them and help them. He sends his Holy Spirit to help us too.

Jesus sometimes called the Holy Spirit 'the Helper'.

Jesus said:

'The Helper will come—the Spirit, who reveals the truth about God... I will send him to you...'
John 15:26

THE HOLY SPIRIT WILL HELP ME.

The Holy Spirit is a wonderful gift from God to every Christian.

The Holy Spirit helps you to know that Jesus loves you.

*T*he Holy Spirit helps you to see the things you do wrong which make Jesus sad.

Things like:

Being unhelpful

Not loving others

I hate him!

Being untruthful

It was him who did it

Being selfish

SWEETS

Being rude

Being bad tempered

Using bad language

OIH NUTTA!

BELONGING...

*I*t's a wonderful feeling when you know that you belong.

Jesus loves us so much that he wants us to belong to God's family.

God's wonderful family is the Christian church.

Its members live all over the world.

It is 2,000 years old.

It will last for ever.

We come from every country.
We are all part of God's
worldwide Church.

As part of God's family we learn to love each other.

WE ENJOY EACH OTHERS COMPANY

WE HELP EACH OTHER

WE PRAY FOR EACH OTHER

WE LOOK AFTER EACH OTHER

Let us be concerned for one another, to help one another to show love and to do good. Let us not give up the habit of meeting together... Let us encourage one another.

Hebrews 10:24–25

25

As part of God's family we learn to be friends with each other.

It's good to meet together with Christian friends to learn about Jesus and to have fun together.

Churches often have special groups where young people can meet together.

Is there a group like this near you?
You could write the name of your group and where it meets here:

....

....

When people don't learn to be friends,
things go wrong.

The bad things in the world make God sad.

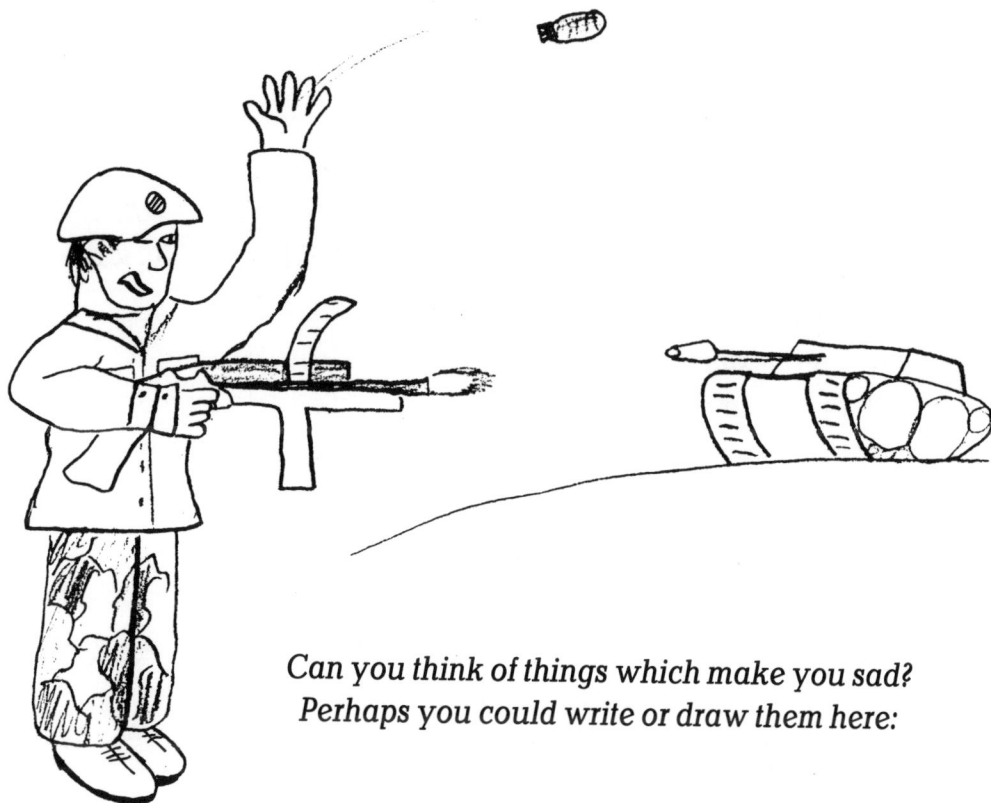

Can you think of things which make you sad?
Perhaps you could write or draw them here:

....

....

....

SOMETHING TO LOOK FORWARD TO...

Isn't it great when you have something to look forward to!

Even though we can't see him now, Jesus promised that one day we shall see him in heaven.

He promised us that we can look forward to being with him for ever.

He says:

'I am the way, the truth, and the life.'

John 14:6

DEAR

· · · · · · · · · · · · · · · · · ·

I LOVE YOU

You can write your name in the space.

SO THIS IS WHAT IT MEANS TO BE A CHRISTIAN!

A Christian is someone who believes in God's Son, Jesus Christ, trusts in his promise, loves him in their heart and shares their life with him.

When you are a Christian:

Jesus shows you that God is like a good and kind Father.

Jesus makes it possible for you to be friends with God for ever.

Jesus gives you his Holy Spirit to help you.

Jesus wants you to know that you are part of God's wonderful family.

Jesus promises us that one day we shall see him in heaven.

Can you find where all these pictures are in the book?

A Christian has something to live for.
A Christian is never alone in the world.
A Christian is safe with God.
A Christian has the best friend ever.

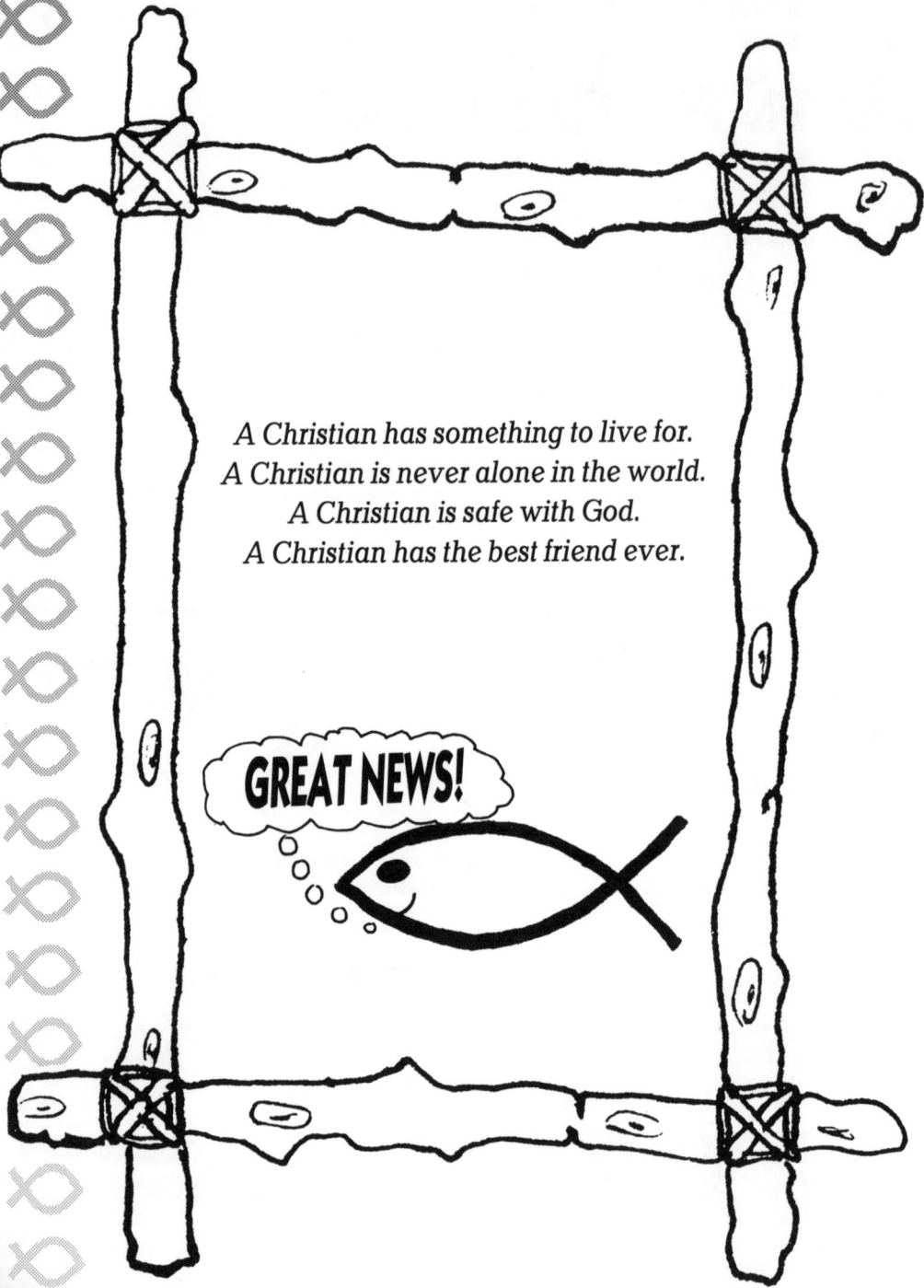

GREAT NEWS!

It's great to be a Christian!

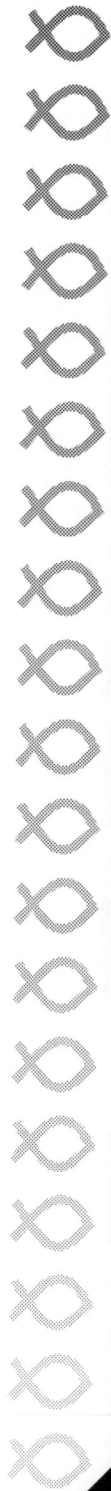

A SPECIAL INVITATION

Now you know what a Christian is, how can you know Jesus for yourself?

When Jesus was on earth he invited people to
come to him.
Jesus gives you the same invitation today.
He wants to be your friend.
He wants you to share your life with him.

Jesus says:
'I will never turn away anyone who come to me.'
John 6:37

When you say 'yes' to Jesus
he forgives you for all the wrong things you have done.

When you say 'yes' to Jesus
he gives you a home in heaven.

When you say 'yes' to Jesus
he gives you his Holy Spirit to help you.

When you say 'yes' to Jesus
you know that you are part of God's wonderful family.

ARE YOU READY FOR THE GREAT ADVENTURE?

Do you want to be a Christian?

THINK CAREFULLY

When you say 'yes' to Jesus you are asking him to be your friend.

Being a Christian means putting Jesus first instead of putting yourself first.

This is not always easy!

But Jesus will help you!

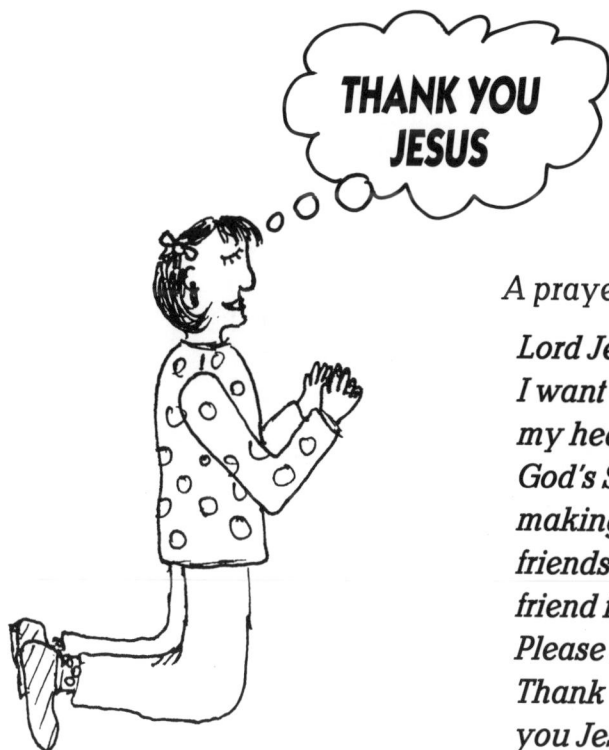

THANK YOU JESUS

A prayer for help:

*Lord Jesus Christ:
I want to be a Christian with all my heart. I believe that you are God's Son. Thank you for making it possible for me to be friends with God. Please be my friend for ever and share my life. Please help me to follow you. Thank you for loving me. Thank you Jesus. Amen*

DOING SOMETHING SPECIAL FOR JESUS

When you become a Christian, Jesus wants you to do something very special. Hold this page up to the mirror to see what it is!

ABOUT TURN!

Jesus wants you to go God's way instead of going your own way.

Jesus wants you to turn away from wrong things.

The Bible calls the wrong things we all think, say and do 'sins'.

Jesus helps you to turn away from your sins.

YOU TURN!

Dear Jesus, Please help me to put right any wrong things I have done. Please help me to say sorry. Amen.

Dear God, Please help me to believe in your Son, Jesus, even when things are hard. Help me to know that you are always close to me. Amen.

Q. Which of these things do you find hard?

Being truthful ☐

Being unselfish ☐

Being helpful ☐

Being generous ☐

Being patient ☐

Being loving ☐

Being obedient ☐

Not being spiteful ☐

Not cheating ☐

Not being sulky ☐

Not being mean ☐

Not being proud ☐

Not lying ☐

Not stealing ☐

Not swearing ☐

THE STORY OF ZACCHAEUS

Zacchaeus was someone who 'about turned'. He used to cheat people, but when he turned to Jesus he found that Jesus changed his life.

Here is the story from Luke's Gospel:

Jesus went on into Jericho and was passing through. There was a chief tax collector there named Zacchaeus, who was rich. He was trying to see who Jesus was, but he was a little man and could not see Jesus because of the crowd. So he ran ahead of the crowd and climbed a sycomore tree to see Jesus, who was going to pass that way. When Jesus came to that place, he looked up and said to Zacchaeus, 'Hurry down, Zacchaeus, because I must stay in your house today.' Zacchaeus hurried down and welcomed him with great joy. All the people who saw it started grumbling. 'This man has gone as a guest to the home of a sinner!' Zacchaeus stood up and said to the Lord, 'Listen, sir! I will give half my belongings to the poor, and if I have cheated anyone, I will pay him back four times as much.' Jesus said to him, 'Salvation has come to this house today, for this man, also, is a descendant of Abraham. The Son of Man came to seek and to save the lost.'

Luke 19:1–10

You could look up the story in your own Bible.

PEOPLE BECOME CHRISTIANS IN DIFFERENT WAYS

Over the past 2,000 years people have become Christians in hundreds of different ways. Some people become Christians suddenly...

The Bible tells us how Saul, who hated Christians, suddenly became a Christian himself on the road to Damascus.
You can read about how this happened in Acts 9:1–31

SOME PEOPLE BECOME CHRISTIANS GRADUALLY...

'I was brought up in a Christian family. From an early age I decided there was probably a God of some sort. I used to think about him, and he gave me a feeling of security. Later I decided that Christianity must be true and that I would follow Jesus. Now I read my Bible day by day and my faith is becoming stronger. I pray that I will keep on growing as a Christian and never give up.'

Peter Martin

*S*ome people become
Christians with the help of
their Christian parents...

or with the help of a Christian
friend...

or when they go to church...

or to a Christian camp...

or to a Holiday Club...

or a Christian group...

or when they read a Christian
book like this one...

Some people don't know exactly when they became
a Christian—they just know that they are!

....

Do you know someone who has become a Christian?

....

How did this person become a Christian?

....

It doesn't matter how you become a Christian.
The great thing is to know that you are a Christian!

39

TRUSTING JESUS

*J*esus wants you to trust him.

To trust Jesus means to rely on him, even when things are hard.

This is what Christians call 'faith'.

I TRUST
THE PILOT

Jesus loves you to talk to him every day.
He loves it when you:

Praise God for all the wonderful
things he has done for you

Really try to turn away from
wrong things

Ask him to help other people
as well as

Yourself

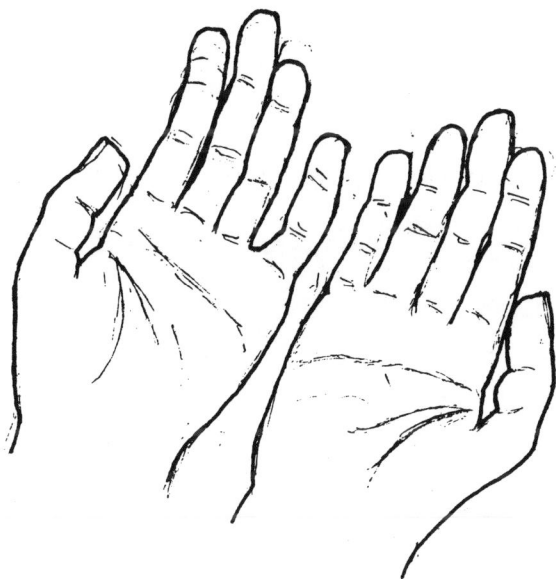

A 'thank you' prayer:

*Dear Jesus, thank you for
helping me to believe in you.
Thank you for helping me to
trust you. Thank you for
being my friend. Please help
me to rely on you.
Amen*

*[God] has given us the very
great and precious gifts he
promised.*

2 Peter 1:4

41

PRAYERS FOR OTHER PEOPLE:

Dear God,

I thank you and I pray for:

People who are close to me:
  family
  friends
  neighbours

People who teach and help me:
  teachers
  leaders
  ministers

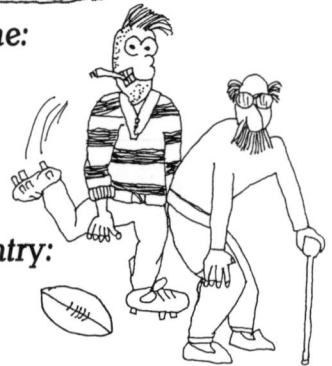

People who look after my country:
  The Queen
  The Prime Minister
  The Government

People who need help in any way:
  patients in hospital
  elderly people
  handicapped people
People who suffer:
  poor people
  homeless people
  hungry people

Special people to pray for:

W e hope you have enjoyed reading this little book and that it has helped you to understand what a Christian is.

Our prayer for you is that if you have begun the Christian adventure you will follow Jesus for the rest of your life.

IT'S GREAT NEWS!

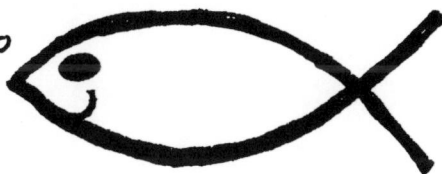

May God, the source of hope, fill you with all joy and peace through your faith in him, so that your hope will grow by the power of the Holy Spirit. For Jesus sake. Amen.

THE BACK PACK

Everything in The Christian Adventure is based on what the Bible tells us about God and about being a Christian. There is lots and lots to find out about God and Jesus. If you are a Christian you are travelling along a road that leads to God and the Bible is your map. Put it in your back pack and take it with you as you go!

Here are some of the things the Bible says which you will find in the pages of this book:

God is always listening – page 2

Psalm 116 starts 'I love the Lord, because he hears me; he listens to my prayers. He listens to me every time I call to him.' It's great to know that God listens to us when we talk to him!

What is a Christian – page 3

Our outward appearance isn't important to God—he looks inside our hearts and there he sees what we are really like. Jesus tells a story about two people, one a very religious person, a Pharisee, who was very proud of all the good things he did. The other person was a tax collector whose job meant people disliked him. But the tax collector loved God and when God looked into the hearts of these two people he could see that the Pharisee only loved himself ... it was the humble tax collector that God listened to. You'll find this story in Luke 18:9–14.

Great news – page 6

In his second letter to his friend, Timothy, Paul says, 'All Scripture [the Bible] is inspired by God and is useful for teaching the truth, rebuking error, correcting faults, and giving instruction for right living, so that the person who serves God may be fully qualified and equipped to do every kind of good deed.' You'll find those words in 2 Timothy 3:16–17. Your Bible will help you find out all about Jesus and how he wants you to live.

In the beginning – page 7

The Bible begins by telling us how God made the world. The story paints a picture of God, the Creator. You'll find this story in Genesis 1. It shows how much God cares for the world he has made.

Wordsearch – page 8

Here is the answer to the wordsearch. The words are really just a few of the wonderful things the Bible says about God. The Book of Psalms has lots of poems and songs which describe God. For example, Psalm 145 is a great hymn of praise. You'll find that it is full of wonderful descriptions of God. Another is Psalm 100 which ends with the words: 'The Lord is good; his love is eternal and his faithfulness lasts for ever.'

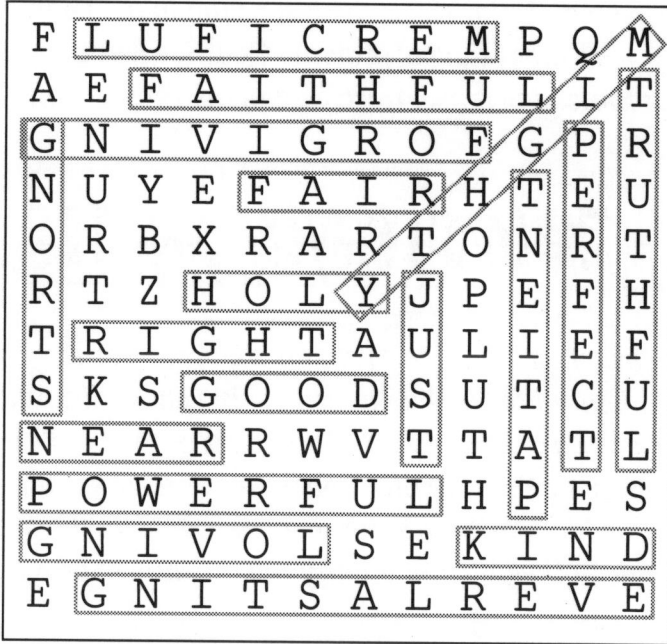

```
F  L  U  F  I  C  R  E  M  P  Q  M
A  E  F  A  I  T  H  F  U  L  I  T
G  N  I  V  I  G  R  O  F  G  P  R
N  U  Y  E  F  A  I  R  H  T  E  U
O  R  B  X  R  A  R  T  O  N  R  T
R  T  Z  H  O  L  Y  J  P  E  F  H
T  R  I  G  H  T  A  U  L  I  E  F
S  K  S  G  O  O  D  S  U  T  C  U
N  E  A  R  R  W  V  T  T  A  T  L
P  O  W  E  R  F  U  L  H  P  E  S
G  N  I  V  O  L  S  E  K  I  N  D
E  G  N  I  T  S  A  L  R  E  V  E
```

What God is like – page 9

In Psalm 103:13 God is described as a very kind father who adores his children: 'As a father is kind to his children, so the Lord is kind to those who honour him.'

When Paul writes to his friend Timothy he describes God as a very wise king: 'To the eternal King, immortal and invisible, the only God—to him be honour and glory for ever!' (1 Timothy 1:17).

You'll find a description of God as a good shepherd in Psalm 23: 'The Lord is my shepherd; I have everything I need' (verse 1).

Praising God – page 10

In the Book of Psalms you will find many, many songs of praise to God. Psalm 150 is the last psalm in the book of Psalms. It's a great song of praise to God. See if you can find it in your Bible. It begins 'Praise God in his Temple!'

The Lord's Prayer – page 12

In the New Testament, in Matthew's Gospel, Jesus tells us that God does not want us to act like big show-offs but to be gentle, caring and forgiving. He teaches us the Lord's Prayer as a pattern for the way that God wants us to talk to him: First of all praising him, then saying we are sorry for the wrong things we have done and finally trusting him to provide our daily needs.

God's Son – page 13

The four Gospel writers—Matthew, Mark, Luke and John— all wrote about Jesus' life on earth. They wrote about things that really happened. At the end of his Gospel, John says, 'Now, there are many other things that Jesus did. If they were all written down one by one, I suppose that the whole world could not hold the books that would be written' (John 21:25).

Jesus' life – page 14

The stories Jesus told are called parables; they always had special meanings. For example, this story about lost sheep is really about how much God loves every single one of us:

'Suppose one of you has a hundred sheep and loses one of them—what do you do? You leave the other ninety-nine sheep in the pasture and go looking for the one that got lost until you find it. When you find it, you are so happy that you put it on your shoulders and carry it back home. Then you call your friends and neighbours together and say to them "I am so happy, I found my lost sheep. Let us celebrate!"'

Luke 15:4–6

Jesus did wonderful things for people. The picture shows him healing a blind man. Here is the story:

Some people brought a blind man to Jesus and begged him to touch him. Jesus took the blind man by the hand and led him out of the village. After spitting on the man's eyes, Jesus placed his hands on him and asked him, 'Can you see anything?' The man looked up and said, 'Yes, I can see people, but they look like trees walking about.' Jesus again placed his hands on the man's eyes. This time the man looked intently, his eyesight returned, and he saw everything clearly.

Mark 8:22–25

Towards the end of his Gospel John says:

In his disciples' presence Jesus performed many other miracles which are not written down in this book. But these have been written in order that you may believe that Jesus is the Messiah, the Son of God, and that through your faith in him you may have life.

John 20:30–31

49

Matthew, Mark, Luke and John tell us about many parables and miracles of Jesus. The Good News Bible sets everything out clearly to make them easy for you to find. It also tells you if that particular incident appears in any of the other Gospels. You can then see how each of the four Gospel writers gave slightly different versions of the same story, depending on how they saw it or heard about it from other people.

Our Father – page 15

John starts his Gospel by telling us who Jesus is. He says, 'No one has ever seen God. The only Son, who is the same as God and is at the Father's side, he has made him known' (John 1:18).

Sometimes even Jesus' close friends found this hard to understand. But Jesus patiently explained to them who he was:

Philip said to him, 'Lord, show us the Father; that is all we need.' Jesus answered, 'For a long time I have been with you all; yet you do not know me, Philip? Whoever has seen me has seen the Father.'

John 14:8–9

Later on he said to another of his friends, Thomas: 'Do you believe because you see me? How happy are those who believe without seeing me!' (John 20:29).

Jesus' death – page 16

John tells us about the wonderful thing that Jesus did for his friend, Lazarus by bringing him back to life after he had died. But then John goes on to tell us about how some of the more powerful people were not pleased about what Jesus was doing:

Many of the people who had come to visit Mary [Lazarus' sister] saw what Jesus did, and they believed in him. But some of them returned to the Pharisees and told them what Jesus had done. So the Pharisees and the chief priests met with the Council and said, 'What shall we do? Look at all the miracles this man is performing! If we let him go on in this way, everyone will believe in him'... From that day on the Jewish authorities made plans to kill Jesus.'

John 11:45–48, 53

They were so narrow-minded that they couldn't see at all who Jesus really was.

Later on Jesus was betrayed by someone who had been his friend. Jesus had gone to a special garden, called Gethsemane, with his friends:

Judas, the traitor, knew where it was, because many times Jesus had met there with his disciples. So Judas went to the garden, taking with him a group of Roman soldiers, and some temple guards sent by the chief priests and the Pharisees; they were armed and carried lanterns and torches. Jesus knew everything that was going to happen to him, so he stepped forward and asked them, 'Who is it you are looking for?' 'Jesus of Nazareth,' they answered. 'I am he,' he said... Then the Roman soldiers with their commanding officer and the Jewish guards arrested Jesus.

John 18:2–4, 12

Each of the four Gospel writers tells us what happened to Jesus after he was arrested and about how he died. Luke says:

The soldiers led Jesus away, and as they were going, they met a man from Cyrene named Simon who was coming into the city from the country. They seized him, put the cross on him, and made him carry it behind Jesus ... When they came to the place called 'The Skull', they crucified Jesus there, and the two criminals, one on his right and the other on his left. Jesus said, 'Forgive them, Father! They don't know what they are doing' ... It was about twelve o'clock when the sun stopped shining and darkness covered the whole country until three o'clock; and the curtain hanging in the Temple was torn in two. Jesus cried out in a loud voice, 'Father! In your hands I place my spirit!' He said this and died.

Luke 23:26, 33–34, 44–46

Jesus' resurrection – page 19

Luke tells us about some of the people who saw Jesus after he rose from the dead. He tells us about two of Jesus' friends who were going to a village called Emmaus. As they were talking about all the things that had happened Jesus himself draw near and walked with them. As they walked along with him they didn't recognize him until, reaching the village, they invited him into the house to eat with them. It was only when he bl____d and broke the bread that at last they recognized ____ ____fter he had gone they said to one another, 'Wasn't it ____ burning in us when he talked to us on the road and ____ the Scriptures to us?'

51

They went quickly back to the others in Jerusalem, where they found that Jesus had also been with Simon Peter. Then, while the two were telling about what had happened to them on the road to Emmaus, 'suddenly the Lord himself stood among them' and said to them 'Peace be with you.' They were terrified, thinking that they were seeing a ghost. But he said to them, 'Why are these doubts coming into your minds? Look at my hands and my feet and see that it is I myself. Feel me, and you will know, for a ghost doesn't have flesh and bones, as you can see I have.' You can read about these events in Luke 24, after the story of the resurrection.

The first Easter – page 20

Jesus knew what was going to happen to him—and why. He knew that it was the only way for us to be be friends with God for ever. The Bible puts it like this:

At one time you were far away from God and were his enemies because of the evil things you did and thought. But now, by means of the physical death of his Son, God has made you his friends, in order to bring you, holy, pure, and faultless, into his presence.

Colossians 1:21–22

When Jesus was telling his friends what was going to happen he said:

'Do not be worried and upset . . . believe in God and believe also in me. There are many rooms in my Father's house, and I am going to prepare a place for you. I would not tell you this if it were not so.'

John 14:1–2

53

Jesus has also prepared a place 'in his Father's house'—in heaven—for you and me.

The Bible says: 'This is what love is: it is not that we have loved God, but that he loved us and sent his Son to be the means by which our sins are forgiven.'

1 John 4:10

When next you are munching your way through a chocolate Easter egg, will you remember what the Bible tells us about the true meaning of Easter? And say thank you to Jesus!

Help on the way – page 22

The Book of Acts in the New Testament tells the story about how the Church began. It was written by the same man, Luke, who wrote the Gospel named after him. In the Book of Acts, he starts by telling us how Jesus went back into heaven, just as Jesus said would. In chapter 2, Luke tells us how the Holy Spirit came to Jesus' friends as they sat together in an upstairs room in a house in Jerusalem. The time when the Holy Spirit first came is known as Pentcost:

When the day of Pentecost came, all the believers were gathered together in one place. Suddenly there was a noise from the sky which sounded like a strong wind blowing, and it filled the whole house where they were sitting. Then they saw what looked like tongues of fire which spread out and touched each person there.

Acts 2:1–3

God, as Jesus had promised, helped Jesus' friends in a very special way to be brave and bold. They told lots of people the truth about Jesus and how he had risen from the dead. As they told more and more people the wonderful news of what

54

God had done, so the new church grew and grew. The Holy Spirit has helped many people to tell others about the wonderful news of Jesus and so God's church continues to grow.

Belonging – page 24

In the New Testament there is a description of God's wonderful family which says it is a body. You could say that some people in the family are 'willing feet', some are 'helping hands', some are 'kind tongues' and some are 'loving arms'. You will find the description of God's Church in 1 Corinthians 12:12–31. Everybody has a part to play in God's wonderful family, no matter who they are or where they live. Verse 27 says: 'All of you are Christ's body, and each one is a part of it.'

Bad things – page 27

From the time he first started to tell people about God, Jesus urged them to turn away from doing bad things:

[He] went to Galilee and preached the Good News from God, 'The right time has come,' he said, 'and the Kingdom of God is near! Turn away from your sins and believe the Good News!'

Mark 1:14–15

John 3:16–17 tells us what the good news is: 'For God loved the world so much that he gave his only Son, so that everyone who believes in him may not die but have eternal life. For God did not send his Son into the world to be its judge, but to be its saviour.' That's great news!

Something to look forward to – page 28

With God's help, through your Bible, your Christian friends and your church, you can start to get to know Jesus right now, here on earth. And you can look forward to being with him for ever. Starting out on the Christian Adventure is the beginning of the rest of your life!

When you to set out on the Christian Adventure you won't be travelling alone because Jesus promises: 'I will be with you always, to the end of the age' (Matthew 28:20). He will travel with you along the road of your life, wherever that may take you.

It's great to be a Christian – page 31

Now that you know what a Christian is, the next part of the book is your special invitation from Jesus. He's longing to be your friend just as soon as you ask him to. You can read through this part of the book whether you feel ready to be friends with Jesus or not—talk it over with your Christian friends or church leaders.

In the last book of the Bible, Jesus says, 'Listen, I stand at the door and knock; if anyone hears my voice and opens the door, I will come in and eat with them, and they with me' (Revelation 3:20).

There is a famous painting of this verse showing Jesus standing at the door of a house with a lamp in his hand. If you look carefully, you will see that there is no handle on the door. When asked about this, the artist replied that the handle was on the inside. Jesus won't push his way into your life. He'll stand at the door and wait for you to ask him in. And when you do then he'll come and be your friend for ever.

THAT'S GREAT NEWS!

Leader's Guide

Your Sunday School teacher or young people's group leader may be interested to know that an action-packed activity pack to accompany this book is available in the UK by sending a second class A5 sae to:

The Bible Reading Fellowship

Peter's Way

Sandy Lane West

Oxford OX4 5HG

Why not ask them to get hold of one?

Jonathan